Guide to
BACKYARD
BIRDS
of the Front Range

Edited by Laura Quattrini

Bird
Conservancy
of the Rockies

Connecting People, Birds and Land

Cover photo by Fernando Boza.

Bird Conservancy
of the Rockies

©2016 Bird Conservancy of the Rockies

ISBN 978-0-692-69913-3
Library of Congress Control Number: 2016906895

Bird Conservancy of the Rockies
14500 Lark Bunting Lane
Brighton, CO 80603

www.birdconservancy.org

MIX
Paper from
responsible sources
FSC   FSC® C021872
www.fsc.org

ACKNOWLEDGEMENTS

Thank you to the following individuals and organizations for donating their time, talents, and knowledge to support this guide:

Wild Birds Unlimited (Fort Collins, Arvada, and Lakewood, Colorado), Jamie Weiss (Audubon Rockies' Habitat Hero Program), Jennifer Renee Meyers, Pamela Smith (Colorado Natural Heritage Program), Jan L. Turner (Colorado Native Plant Society), Theodore Parker-Renga, Dr. Nathan D. Pieplow and students (University of Colorado Boulder), Cornell Lab of Ornithology, Paul Caputo (National Association for Interpretation), and Bird Conservancy of the Rockies staff.

Thank you to the following organizations for sponsoring the development of this guide:

Wild Birds Unlimited (three stores in Colorado)
Fort Collins http://fortcollins.wbu.com
Arvada http://northmetro.wbu.com
Lakewood http://denver.wbu.com

Denver Museum of Nature & Science
http://www.dmns.org

Audubon Rockies' Habitat Hero Program
http://rockies.audubon.org/conservation/habitat-hero-education

Sterling Ranch
http://sterlingranchcolorado.com

National Association for Interpretation
http://www.interpnet.com

Rotary Club of Fort Collins
http://www.rotarycluboffortcollins.org

Scientific and Cultural Facilities District
http://scfd.org

We give a special thanks to all the photographers who have given us permission to use their photos.

Contents

Hairy Woodpecker

Introduction

The Rocky Mountain Front is a unique geologic area in western North America where the Rocky Mountains transition to the Great Plains. It stretches from Mexico to Canada, with the most dramatic geologic area being the Front Range Mountains of central Colorado north to central Wyoming and south to northern New Mexico. The relatively flat shortgrass prairie rises nearly 10,000 feet above the prairie floor to form foothills and lofty mountaintops, such as Pikes Peak and Longs Peak that both reach more than 14,000 feet above sea level. This varying topography of the Front Range holds a biologically rich set of ecosystems. Grasslands, shrublands, wetlands, and forests each consist of their own natural communities with plants, animals, and other forms of life unique to each ecosystem.

JON DELORENZO

View of Flatirons
from Standley Lake,
Westminster, CO

Casper

Wyoming

Cheyenne

Denver

Colorado

Pueblo

New Mexico

Santa Fe

Sources: Esri, USGS, NOAA

EMILY GUBLER

European settlers started inhabiting the Front Range in the early 1800s, drawn to the region for hunting and trading. The growth of industries including mining, agriculture, railroad building, manufacturing, and technology has continuously brought people to the area. In addition, the Front Range offers a myriad of opportunities for recreation including birding, fishing, hiking, biking, climbing, camping, and skiing. As a result, the Front Range is the most heavily urbanized area of the United States between Chicago and the West Coast. This widespread and rapid suburban and commercial development is the primary threat to natural areas along the Front Range and the wildlife they support.

For birds—especially birds that migrate—this development has introduced numerous threats to their survival, from power lines to domesticated cats to decreased habitat on their wintering and breeding grounds and migratory stopover sites. This has led to local and continental population declines for many bird species. Concerned about the loss of our birds, numerous people, organizations, and agencies are working to reverse these declining population trends and keep common bird species common. After all, birds serve as indicators of a healthy natural world because they are highly sensitive to environmental changes and their populations reflect the overall environmental health.

At Bird Conservancy of the Rockies, our mission is to conserve birds and their habitats. We work to raise awareness of the plight of our feathered friends and engage people, like you, in conservation, so we can ensure our birds exist for generations to come.

By following tips in this guide and learning about birds of the Front Range, you can help us conserve birds and their habitats! Simple actions can be easy to do, yet make a big impact. The actions we take can have a significant effect on birds and other wildlife that share the habitat with us. Whether you have an apartment balcony or many acres of land, you can start by adding plants and other components to your space that can provide habitat for birds. This can be as simple as installing a water feature or bird feeder or as involved as planting native trees and shrubs. Enhancing your yard is something you can do at any age, and you can go at your own pace. Not only can you attract birds and other wildlife by doing this, but you can create a unique and visually appealing environment for you. In addition, you can set an example for visitors to your yard, especially young children, who will learn the basics of nature appreciation. Who knows? This may evolve into a lifelong passion for birds!

Bird Conservancy
of the Rockies

Native flowers in a
Colorado backyard

PAUL CAPUTO

How To Use This Guide

This guide will provide you with information on creating an ideal habitat for birds and identifying birds of the Front Range. To get the most out of this guide, follow these steps:

1. Learn how to be a good steward of our birds

2. Determine the ecosystem in which you live

3. Understand the four basic needs of birds

4. Plan and create your bird sanctuary

5. Supplement what nature provides in your yard

6. Understand the ethics and etiquette of birding

7. Learn to identify bird species and keep a checklist

8. Get additional resources on bird conservation

Safety First
BE A GOOD STEWARD OF OUR BIRDS

Before you begin planning your bird refuge, make sure that you are not endangering birds by drawing them to potential threats in your yard. Get to know possible dangers and how to avoid or reduce them to ensure the safety of birds.

CATS

Cats present one of the biggest dangers to wild birds. Free-ranging felines kill up to 4 billion birds every year in the United States. The bacteria in cat saliva are toxic to birds, so even if a cat does not immediately kill a bird, its bite can lead to infection and death for the bird.

What to do: The best way to keep your cat from hunting birds and other wildlife is to keep it indoors. This is safer for both your pet and wild birds. If you must let your cat outside and can't keep an eye on it yourself, take the following precautions to minimize danger.

- Shorten the amount of time spent outside. This is less time your cat has to "play" with wildlife. Birds are most active at dusk and dawn. These would be the best times to keep your cat inside.

- Trim your cat's claws to make it harder to climb trees.

- Don't feed feral cats. This encourages them to stay in your yard.

- Spay or neuter your cat. While this will not affect its hunting behavior, it will keep your cat from adding to cat populations.

- Go shopping! You can find a number of different products, such as colorful cat collars, cat bibs, and pens to keep cats contained, that claim to lessen the ability of your cat to catch wildlife.

WINDOWS

Windows reflect the sky and trees, which birds see. Instead of flying into their apparent habitat, they strike the window. Window collisions can kill birds on contact, but even injured birds may develop fatal internal injuries or become easy targets for predators. American Bird Conservancy (ABC) has an entire Glass Collisions Program devoted to the subject. The suggestions below are based on their recommendations.

What to do:

- To minimize the threat of glass make it more visible. Many homeowner products such as ABC BirdTape™, blinds, films and adhesives have been shown to significantly reduced bird collisions. You can see how they rate and where to get them at www.abcbirds.org/get-involved/bird-smart-glass/.

- Add designs, decals, sun catchers, or wind chimes to the outside of windows to break up reflections. Follow the 2 X 4 rule suggested by ABC in which horizontal spaces should be no more than 2 inches apart and/or vertical spaces should be no more than 4 inches apart (many songbirds don't try to fly through spaces smaller than this size).

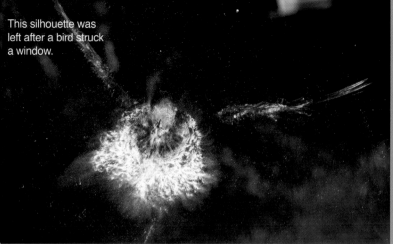

This silhouette was left after a bird struck a window.

BILL GRACEY

- Place feeders at appropriate locations. If you want your feeder near a window, locate it within 3 feet so when birds take off they cannot build enough momentum to injure themselves against the glass. If placed farther away from the window (at least 30 feet), feeders should be near shrubbery, so birds are more likely to fly to the closest "real" habitat.

- Avoid visual tunnels, or windows on opposite walls. Birds think they can fly through the open space created by both openings. Close doors or draw shades to eliminate these spaces.

- Keep "shelter" items, such as houseplants, away from windows.

- Partially close blinds to produce the vertical or horizontal lines (thereby achieving the 2 X 4 rule).

- Using awnings, overhangs, curtains, etc. is not significantly effective at reducing reflections.

DIRTY EQUIPMENT

Dirty equipment, such as bird feeders, birdbaths, and birdhouses, breed bacteria and mold and attract pests dangerous to birds' health.

What to do:

- Get in the habit of regularly cleaning out your feeders, baths, and other equipment at least once a month. How often you clean a piece of equipment depends on how many birds use it. A more popular feeder may need to be cleaned more often. Hummingbird feeders should be cleaned every few days.

- Look for signs of food spoilage. As with equipment, food and nectar can go bad and cause bacteria and mold to grow. Make sure food stays dry and nectar remains fresh.

- Use a solution of 1 part bleach to 9 parts water, dish detergent, or a commercial cleaner when cleaning equipment.

- Rinse equipment thoroughly with plain water to remove any chemicals.

- Wait for parts to dry completely before reassembling or filling with food.

OAKLEY ORIGINALS

Nectar in a feeder should be checked daily to ensure it is not spoiled.

- Consider using equipment made with antimicrobial materials, which inhibit the growth of bacteria and mold on surfaces.

- Clean areas around bird feeders. Leftover seed on the ground can also spoil and attract pests.

JUNK FOOD

Junk food is a problem for birds, too! Different birds have different dietary requirements. These nutritional needs are especially important to developing hatchlings.

What to do:

- Don't feed birds human junk food. It's not necessarily good for us, and it's definitely not good for birds. Avoid foods such as potato chips, white bread, and cookies.

- Check what is in your bird food blend. Most commercial mixes contain a high percentage of milo (a seed, also called sorghum) and other fillers that most birds do not like.

- Tailor your bird food to the species you want to bring to your feeder. Check out the Bird Food section on page 42 of this guide for healthy food preferences.

MICHELLE TRIBE

PESTICIDES

Pesticides (including herbicides and insecticides), even in small quantities, are dangerous to birds, especially if birds are eating and grooming on the ground or where pesticides have been sprayed.

What to do:

- Consider how important the need is for pesticides in your yard. A wild backyard is even more appealing to native birds.

- Switch to environmentally friendly pest control methods. Non-chemical controls may include biological controls or mechanical measures, such as pulling and chopping. Parisitoids (some wasps and flies), pathogens (bacteria, viruses, and fungi), predators (beetles, true bugs, spiders, and wasps), and weed-feeders can be important natural controls of some insect pests and weeds.

Despite all of our best efforts, accidents do happen. If you find an injured bird, do not try to care for the bird yourself. Call a local licensed wildlife rehabilitator, state wildlife agency (Colorado Parks and Wildlife or Wyoming Game and Fish Department), or wildlife veterinarian as soon as possible. If you need to transfer the bird to a rehabilitator or keep it safe until someone can get to you, find a box or paper bag to put the bird in and keep the box or bag taped or clipped shut. Keep the box or bag in a warm, dark location and safe from children or pets. Do not bother the bird as it will simply stress it out.

If you find a baby bird, try to let nature take its course. Unless the bird is obviously injured, leave the bird alone. Fledglings (young birds that are fully feathered and "fuzzy" looking) often leave the nest to explore—it's vital for the bird's development. You can help it by giving it space and making sure your pets don't get to it. A bird that is unfeathered (hatchling) or with only a few pin feathers (nestling) most likely fell out of its nest. If you can find the nest (look up!), you can pick the bird up and put

Fledgling Western Scrub-Jay

it back into the nest. If the nest blew out of a tree or shrub, gently pick up the nest and place it where it was if you can safely do so. Birds have a poor sense of smell, so it's a myth birds will abandon their young once handled by people.

Plant Communities
DETERMINE THE ECOSYSTEM IN WHICH YOU LIVE

The Front Range consists of an area that rises thousands of feet in elevation. As you go up in elevation, the vegetation changes. At lower elevations along the Front Range, you find more grasslands. As the elevation increases, you find more shrublands, eventually transitioning to more coniferous forests at higher elevations. Interspersed within these varying plant communities are wetlands, or areas around rivers, lakes and streams, with their own vegetation types. Determining the ecosystem in which you live will help you design a successful bird sanctuary in your yard, so you pick appropriate plants that will thrive. Also, different plant communities provide suitable habitat for different birds, so knowing the ecosystem in which you live will help you know what bird species you can expect to find.

GRASSLANDS

Short Grasses

Historically, flat lands along the Front Range have consisted largely of short-stature grasses, including blue grama and buffalo grass. While much of the shortgrass prairie along the Front Range has been converted to agricultural and urban areas within the last century, pockets of native prairie can still be found on the eastern edge of the Front Range. These extremely drought resistant grasses used to dominate this ecosystem and can be found up to 6,000 feet. Trees are rarely found within this plant community, except for wetter areas where the plains cottonwood thrives, providing important habitat for birds and other wildlife. It should be noted that grassland bird species are one of the fastest declining groups of birds in North America.

Pawnee National Grasslands with native flowers.

Tall Grasses

High-stature grasses, including little bluestem and needle and thread grasses, exist within a relatively narrow elevation band between the shortgrass prairie

BIRD SPECIES
- Horned Lark
- Vesper Sparrow
- Western Meadowlark

and shrublands and forests of the foothills. Increased moisture in the soil allows for mixed and tall grasses to thrive on moderate to gentle slopes between 5,200 and 7,200 feet. Fire suppression along the Front Range has allowed for shrubs and trees to invade these grasslands, altering habitat for birds and other wildlife. Much of the tall grass plant community along the Front Range has also been altered by agricultural and urban development, so it is unusual to find healthy occurrences of this ecosystem here.

Gambel oak

SHRUBLANDS

This plant community can exist at elevations from 5,000 to 9,500 feet. Shrublands vary in density and may include Gambel oak, mountain mahogany, skunkbrush sumac, and antelope bitterbrush. Some shrubs, such as black chokecherry, can grow quite large. Shrublands are sometimes interspersed with trees or patches of grass.

BIRD SPECIES
- Broad-tailed Hummingbird
- Say's Phoebe
- Western Scrub-Jay
- Spotted Towhee
- Black-headed Grosbeak
- Lazuli Bunting
- American Goldfinch

CHARLES M. SAUE

FORESTS

Pinyon-Juniper Woodlands
This plant community is dominated by two species of conifers: pinyon pine and/or juniper. Occurring in a limited distribution along the south end of the Front Range, these trees can be found on the lower parts of the foothills at elevations between 4,900 and 8,000 feet. Trees are relatively short (usually less than 20 feet tall) and are often mixed with other plant communities including shrublands and grasslands.

Ponderosa Pine Woodlands
This prevalent plant community is common between 6,000 and 8,000 feet. Ponderosa pine trees are drought resistant. This ecosystem can have understory plants (shrubs and grasses) that add to the bird diversity found here.

BIRD SPECIES
- Great Horned Owl
- Northern Flicker
- Hairy Woodpecker
- Western Wood-Pewee
- Warbling Vireo
- Black-capped Chickadee
- Brown Creeper
- White-breasted Nuthatch
- Western Tanager
- Dark-eyed Junco
- Pine Siskin

WETLANDS

Wetlands are areas along rivers, lakes, and streams. This plant community has the highest plant and animal diversity among ecosystems along the Front Range because of the presence of water. Wetlands can vary from marshes (always flooded) with cattails and bulrushes, to wet meadows (periodically flooded) with low grasses and sedges, to flowing streams, rivers, and ponds, each with differing types of vegetation including plains cottonwood, American plum, snowberry, and willow species.

BIRD SPECIES
- Eastern Screech-Owl
- Downy Woodpecker
- Black-capped Chickadee
- House Wren
- Yellow Warbler
- Yellow-breasted Chat
- Red-winged Blackbird
- Brown-headed Cowbird
- Bullock's Oriole

Four Basic Needs of Birds
PROVIDE FOOD, WATER, SHELTER, & A PLACE TO NEST

Birds visit or settle in an area based on how well that area fulfills its requirements. An ideal bird habitat meets four basic needs: food, water, shelter, and a place to nest and raise young. To create an ideal habitat for birds in your yard and to increase the likelihood that our feathered friends use it, you should provide one or more of these elements. Learning more about what each bird species requires or prefers can help you tailor the plan for your bird sanctuary to attract certain species.

In a time of increasing urban sprawl and habitat fragmentation, you can help conserve bird species by providing a wider diversity of these resources for birds. This will be especially important for birds that travel thousands of miles during spring and fall migration. These birds are expecting their route to have adequate refueling habitat for their journey but instead find miles and miles of urban and suburban houses and yards. A yard that offers food, shelter, and water can make the difference between life and death for birds as they make their semiannual treks.

This American Robin found its basic needs for raising young.

FOOD

Create a natural environment in your yard to provide the best and most diverse sources of food for birds. A healthy backyard ecosystem provides relationships between plants and wildlife that form a food web. At the basic level, primary producers (plants) provide energy (food) that attracts consumers (birds

and other wildlife). A bird's dietary requirements and food sources will also be different at different time of year. Insects comprise an extremely critical part of the food web for birds during the spring, summer (about 96% of terrestrial birds feed their young insects). Berries and seeds from trees, shrubs, and grasses will be important in the fall and winter to prepare birds for migration and for birds who stay through the winter. Growing native plants is the best way to provide those plant and animal food sources. However, you can supplement naturally occurring food by providing bird feeding stations.

WATER

Provide water sources in your yard. Water is second only to food in the number of species it attracts.

It is especially important to provide an open water source when all else is frozen. Birds will bathe in sub-freezing temperatures. It is essential that they keep their feathers clean and fluffed, which enables them to more efficiently trap insulating air next to their bodies to keep warm. Open water also quenches their thirst while ingesting snow can actually lead to dehydration.

MAHAK MITTAL

SHELTER AND A PLACE TO NEST

Design your bird sanctuary with places for birds to seek shelter. When you look at an aerial photograph of suburban and urban areas, what do you see? Houses and yards usually are what stand out. While one yard may be small, together, many houses with wildlife habitat have the potential to become a larger island or stepping stone of habitat getting a bird that much closer to the next patch of habitat. These patches can provide crucial resources to maintain healthy bird populations.

Offer a suitable place for birds to nest and raise young if you want to welcome the joy of babies into your yard. Backyard vegetation including trees, shrubs, and un-mowed grasses can serve this purpose well. See the following sections for incorporating natural habitat or artificial nest boxes into your space.

Creating Your Bird Sanctuary

PLAN & IMPLEMENT AN IDEAL HABITAT FOR BIRDS

These are considerations you need to make before planning a wildlife haven in your yard.

Note:
Check in with your HOA covenants or city ordinances to make sure you are complying before you start the planning process. This will save time, money and headaches down the road.

Audubon Rockies 2015
Residential Garden Habitat
Hero contest winner.

INA DUFFY

Assess soils and drainage.

In the western United States, many challenges exist for establishing new plants. Most of our soils are made of heavy clay, which have poor aeration that limits root growth. If you have poor soil (heavy clay, dusty, or lacking nutrients), it may be worth the extra time and money to improve the quality of the soil before you put plants in the ground. Soil amendments are materials added to a soil to improve its physical properties. The best way to improve a clay or sandy soil is to add organic matter, which helps break up the soil for better air and water penetration, and increases its water-holding capacity. In areas with poor soil drainage, consider building mounds, berms, or raised planters. Too much standing water can make plant roots rot.

Determine sun exposure.

Consider how much sun a plant needs. A plant requiring full sun will not do well in mostly shaded areas. In addition, areas in full sun get dried out faster. Consider the maintenance required to grow plants in certain areas of your yard and whether you'd need an irrigation system.

Mitigate for wildfires.

Depending on where you reside along the Front Range, you may live in an area where a high potential for wildfire exists. While wildfires are a natural part of the environment, you should adapt the area around your house so that, if a fire burns, firefighters can do their job safely to protect you and your property. In addition, you should have a defensible space around your home or other structures in which the environment has been modified to lessen fire hazard, which involves reducing the fuels (vegetation, brush, and wood piles) close to structures. Check with your county and local state forester for information on how to mitigate fuels surrounding your home.

Map out your yard.

Knowing what dimensions you have to work with for various yard climates (sunny vs. shady areas, wetter vs. drier areas) and sketching in the play areas and walkways will help you pick out the right-sized plants for the right places. Seeking the assistance of a landscape architect can be an initial financial burden but provide you with a solid plan for your yard.

Check with your city or county to see if they offer rebates for hiring a landscape architect to help you plan your yard.

If you don't have much of a yard, you can grow many native plants in containers. Plus, by doing this, you have the added advantage of moving around plants if you don't like their original locations. To be eco-wise and keep costs low, look for items around your house or at yard sales that can be repurposed as plant containers. But make sure the containers will have enough drainage.

A map of your yard can be as simple as a home drawing.

Plan for birds and YOU.

Native plants are great for birds, but sometimes plants can help you achieve other goals in addition to attracting and supporting wildlife. Do you want more color in your yard? Plants can provide an entire spectrum of colors from their flowers, leaves, and branches. Is there an area of your yard that you would like shaded, or where you'd like to block the view? Planting a tree or shrub can help you achieve that. Be thoughtful on plant placement, however, and carefully consider how you use the different areas of your yard. Do you have play areas or pathways? You probably don't want to plant a bush right in the middle of that area. Is there a view you enjoy? Do not plant a tree in between you and that view. Think about the overall picture of how you want your yard to function.

Call before you dig!

Be safe when digging holes for placing larger plants. Also, consider how deep roots might grow – you may not want to plant a tree right over a septic tank. Dial 811 about a week before digging to schedule a locator to mark any underground utility lines in your yard.

RICK/BRENDA BEERHOF

PICK YOUR PLANTS

Go with natives.

Native plants such as milkweed attract more than just birds. Insects, like this monarch butterfly, also benefit.

Beyond just supporting wildlife, native plants are beautiful, increase scenic value, and thrive in the habitat in which they have evolved. The harsh climate conditions of the Front Range—due to elevation, scant precipitation, wind, clayey soils, and extreme day-to-day and seasonal temperature fluctuations—make for less-than-ideal growing conditions. Native plants are adapted to an arid ecosystem and won't require large amounts of water once they are established. They also require less maintenance, fertilizers, and pesticides than other ornamentals. Thus, if you plant with hardy natives, your plants will be easier to grow and maintain.

Time your plants.

The relationship between birds and native plants is specialized to sync up with nutritional demands at different times of the year. For instance, birds that are getting ready for winter stock up on fall berries, such as chokecherry and golden currant, that are higher in fat to help them "plump up" to stay warm during the colder months that lie ahead. Sunflower seeds and acorns are another good source of fat for the winter. Compare that to summer berries with high sugar content, which help with keeping up with higher energy demands for raising a clutch.

Consider birds' needs throughout the year and how plant bloom time and succession can provide food and cover for as long a period as possible. Early blooming plants feed hungry insects, and these insects feed hungry baby birds. Spring and summer blooms will sustain birds throughout the rest of the season. Berries and seeds will feed birds during the fall and winter. Having trees and shrubs that provide cover can attract cold birds looking for shelter.

Attract the right birds.

Plants are great alluring advertisers, as they need to rely on wildlife to pollinate them so they have successful offspring to perpetuate another generation. Plants advertise via smell, patterns, color, and markings, all of which are recognized by birds that have evolved alongside these native plants. Therefore, certain plants will attract certain birds. Are there any particular bird species you want to see in your yard or other space? Learn the habitat and food needs of these birds and whether specific plants can provide for them. See the Species Profiles section of this guide for more.

It's worth noting that some bird species are generalists and can take advantage of a variety of different resources in a wide variety of environmental conditions. These species aren't picky about what they eat or where they live. When environmental conditions change, generalists are able to adapt. In fact, when placed into an unfamiliar environment, not within their native range, generalists can quickly take hold, thrive, and increase in numbers. They can even out-compete native bird species. On the other hand, some bird species are specialists that can only thrive in a narrow range of environmental conditions. Many specialists have evolved anatomical features that limit what they can eat, such as hummingbirds. Most bird species fall somewhere between the generalist-specialist spectrum.

Examples of Native Trees Along the Front Range

Trees	Drought tolerant	Scientific name	Wildlife use and other notes
Plains Cottonwood		*Populus deltoides/ monilifera*	Cover* for birds; supports insects; note: cottonwoods need extra water
Pinyon Pine	✓	*Pinus edulis*	Cover for birds; fruit (seeds) for birds
Rocky Mountain Juniper	✓	*Sabina scopulorum*	Cover for birds; fruit for birds; note: there are male and female junipers. Female plants bear fruit; males produce pollen and no fruit.
Ponderosa Pine	✓	*Pinus ponderosa*	Cover for birds; fruit (seeds) for birds

* Cover indicates shelter and nesting substrates for birds.

Cedar Waxwing enjoying juniper berries.

RICHARD HURD

Examples of Native Bushes/Shrubs Along the Front Range

Bushes/shrubs	Drought tolerant	Scientific name	Wildlife use and other notes
Gambel Oak	✓	*Quercus gambelii*	Cover for birds; attracts insects; fruit (seeds) for birds
Netleaf Hackberry	✓	*Celtis reticulata*	Fruit for birds
Hawthorn	✓	*Crataegus erythropoda*	Cover for birds; fruit for birds
Western Sandcherry	✓	*Prunus besseyi*	Cover for birds; fruit for birds; supports insects; note: fragrant flowers
Black Choke-cherry		*Prunus virginiana melanocarpa*	Cover for birds; fruit for birds; supports insects
American Plum		*Prunus americana*	Cover for birds; fruit for birds; supports insects
Antelope Bitterbush	✓	*Purshia tridentata*	Cover for birds; supports insects (great for bees); deer and other big game like to eat this plant
Rubber Rabbitbrush	✓	*Chrysothamnus nauseosus*	Supports moths, butterflies, and birds; note: attractive winter form; reproduces vigorously; blooms later than many plants
Skunkbush Sumac	✓	*Rhus aromatic trilobata*	Cover for birds; fruit for birds
Golden Currant		*Ribes aureum odoratum*	Cover for birds; fruit and nectar for birds; note: wonderful fragrance—like cloves

Bushes/ shrubs	Drought tolerant	Scientific name	Wildlife use and other notes
Boulder Raspberry		*Oreobatus deliciosus*	Fruit for birds
Thimbleberry		*Rubacer parviflorus*	Fruit for birds
Snowberry		*Symphoricar-pos albus*	Cover for birds; fruit for birds
Willow species		*Salix* spp.	Cover for birds; supports insects (nectar for bees, host for larval butterflies); note: willows like moist areas
Apache Plume	✓	*Fallugia paradoxa*	Cover for birds; supports insects (host for larval butterflies)
Yucca	✓	*Yucca glauca*	Supports insects; nectar, seeds and nesting material for birds
Red-Osier Dogwood		*Swida sericia*	Fruit for birds; note: tolerates some shade

This red-osier dogwood has marvelous fall colors and beautiful spring flowers

MATT LAVIN

ANDREY ZARHKIKI

Examples of Native Perennials Along the Front Range

Perennials	Drought tolerant	Scientific name	Wildlife use and other notes
Bush Sunflower		*Helianthus pumilus*	Fall seed source; good for insects
Stemless Evening-Primrose	✓	*Oenothera caespitosa*	Nectar for moths, seed for birds; Note: fragrant white flowers
Howard's Evening-Primrose	✓	*Oenothera howardii*	Nectar for moths, seed for birds; Note: fragrant yellow flowers
Orange Butterfly-weed	✓	*Asclepias tuberosa*	Host for larval butterflies including Monarchs*; nectar for insects
Showy Milkweed	✓	*Asclepias speciosa*	Host for larval butterflies including Monarchs*; nectar for insects; fragrant ball of pink flowers
Swamp Milkweed	✓	*Asclepias incarnata*	Host for larval butterflies including Monarchs*; nectar for insects
Prairie Coneflower	✓	*Ratibida columnifera*	Seed source for birds; attracts insects
Yellow Prickly Pear	✓	*Opuntia polyacantha*	Nectar and pollen for insects; seeds for birds; Note: may become weedy or invasive in some areas

Perennials	Drought tolerant	Scientific name	Wildlife use and other notes
Big Root Prickly Pear	✓	*Opuntia macrorhiza*	Nectar and pollen for insects; seeds and fruit for birds
Wild Four O'clock	✓	*Mirabilis multiflora*	Nectar feeding insects
Rocky Mountain Bee Plant		*Cleome serrulata*	Nectar for insects; seed for some birds
Rocky Mountain Penstemon	✓	*Penstemon strictus*	Nectar for insects; seed for some birds
Scarlet Bugler Penstemon	✓	*Penstemon barbatus*	Nectar for insects; seed for some birds
Silvery Lupine	✓	*Lupinus argenteus*	Nectar for insects; seed for some birds
Colorado Columbine		*Aquilegia caerulea*	Attracts bees

Rocky mountain bee plant.

Perennials	Drought tolerant	Scientific name	Wildlife use and other notes
Lance-leaf Coreopsis		*Coreopsis lanceolata*	Seed for birds
Rocky Mountain Iris		*Iris missouriensis*	Nectar for insects; Note: likes areas that are wet part of the time
Pasque Flowers		*Anemone patens*	Nectar for insects
Prairie Smoke		*Geum triflorum*	Nectar for insects
Golden Banner	✓	*Thermopsis divaricarpa*	Nectar for insects; bumble bees like it
Bee Balm; Horsemint; Wild Bergamot		*Monarda fistulosa*	Hummingbirds; bees
Gayfeather		*Liatris punctata*	Insects; Note: blooms very late in season; rose pink

* Monarch butterfly populations are declining.

Lance-leaf coreopsis.

ALVIN KHO

Examples of Native Grasses Along the Front Range

Grasses	Drought tolerant	Scientific name	Wildlife use and other notes
Indian Grass		*Sorghastrum avenaceum*	Seed source for birds
Little Bluestem	✓	*Schizachyrium scoparium*	Seed source for birds
Side Oats Grama Grass	✓	*Bouteloua curtipendula*	Seed source for birds
Blue Grama	✓	*Chondrosum bouteloua gracilis*	Seed source for birds
Indian Ricegrass	✓	*Achnatherum hymenoides*	Seed source for birds
Needle-and-Thread	✓	*Hesperostipa comata*	Seed source for birds
Buffalo Grass	✓	*Buchloe dactyloides*	Seed source for birds

To find more native plants, visit a local, reputable plant nursery or check out resources on the internet. Websites of the Colorado and New Mexico Native Plant Societies and Wyoming Wildscape have suggested lists of native plants to be used for gardens in Colorado and Wyoming, as well as links to other resources. If you don't want to select specific plants, Audubon Rockies' Habitat Hero Program has partnered with High Country Gardens to create pre-planned gardens in a box. The Center for Resource Conservation also has xeric gardens in a box. Check out the Bird Conservation Resources section of this guide for information on these organizations and others that can help you select native plants.

Buffalo grass can be used to create a drought-resistant turf for your yard.

WILDBIRDS UNLIMIT

ARRANGE YOUR PLANTS AND YARD FEATURES

Birds select habitat based on both horizontal and vertical structure in addition to the types of plants. Make sure your plants have enough room to grow between each other but also consider how a bird might use the plants. If it's for shelter, planting shrubs closer together to form a thicket may be useful. Also consider how plants will grow vertically as this will increase the amount of space some birds can utilize. Taller native shrubs and trees, including dead trees or snags, will offer shelter and nesting area needed to protect some birds from weather and predators. Grassland bird species, on the other hand, have no interest in being near trees as they often harbor predator species.

As you prune and care for your bird sanctuary consider uses for the debris. Arrange brush piles in your yard as an inexpensive way to provide shelter and additional benefits for birds, such as nesting material and attracting insects. Pile up leaves, sticks, tree limbs, and some grass cuttings in the corner of your yard. You've just addressed the shelter and food elements to your backyard bird habitat!

Consider Maintenance Needs

Determine how the plants in your yard or other space need to be maintained and how much time you have to take care of them. While most native plants are more drought-tolerant, they do need a lot of watering to get established. Consider the need for an irrigation system. New garden beds also usually will grow a lot of weeds after you work the soil. Be prepared to control the weeds. Mulching can help you deal with both of these issues and has the added benefit of encouraging insects.

Certify Your Yard!

Once you get a bird sanctuary going in your yard, take it a step further by certifying it. The National Wildlife Federation (NWF) will certify your yard if you provide sources of food, water, shelter, and nesting locations. NWF has an active community of more than 400,000 people with certified yards across the United States! Other groups that will give your garden the distinguished designation it deserves include Audubon Rockies' Habitat Hero Program and North American Butterfly Association's Butterfly Garden Certification Program.

OTHER CONSIDERATIONS

Determine how much money you have to spend initially to get your bird sanctuary going. From site preparation to maintenance, you may have to pay for more than just plants and equipment. Start small and expand over time to keep the financial burden low. Buying stock plants can be expensive, so save money by starting plants from seed but understand it does take extra diligence. Growing the footprint of a native garden over time keeps it more manageable as plants gradually get established.

Feeders, Food, Water Sources & Birdhouses

SUPPLEMENT WHAT NATURE PROVIDES

Sometimes you may not have the space or be able to build an ideal habitat in your yard. You may want to supplement what nature provides to attract birds. You can provide feeders, bird food, water sources, and birdhouses to do this.

Attract eye-catching bird species such as these American Goldfinches, Black-headed Grosbeaks, and Lazuli Buntings.

FEEDERS

A good bird feeder is essential for healthy eating. You can find instructions online to build a simple feeder yourself, or buy one from a reputable backyard bird store. Not all species will eat from a feeder. Learn more about the species you are trying to attract to specialize your feeding stations.

Types of feeders

There are many types of bird feeders, and the kind you choose will determine the type of birds you attract and how often you will need to clean it.

■ Tray/platform feeders: These are the simplest feeders and can be easily made or purchased from a store. They attract the widest variety of birds. Since these trays are open, seeds are more vulnerable to spoiling from exposure to rain, snow, and bird droppings, so they should be replaced more often. In addition, these feeders offer no protection against squirrels.

■ Hopper feeders: These feeders attract a wide range of birds and can contain enough seed to last for days, so they do not have to be refilled as often. With walls and a roof, they offer more protection against moisture. However, if water does make it inside, it can be a breeding ground for mold and bacteria. These feeders are also extremely attractive to squirrels.

- Tube feeders: These hollow, cylindrical feeders can be made of mesh wire or plastic with metal feeding ports. These feeders are good for attracting smaller birds, while preventing larger birds such as jays from feeding. The plastic tube feeders may be squirrel resistant. The best tube feeders have feeding ports at the very end of the tube, thus preventing seed buildup at the bottom.

- Window feeders: These plastic feeders attach to glass or hook onto window frames, allowing you to see birds close-up. They are the most likely feeders to prevent window collisions, but can be easily accessed by squirrels.

- Specialty feeders: Examples of specialty feeders include suet feeders and hummingbird feeders. These each have specific cleaning and refilling directions.

Squirrel baffles

These handy accessories protect your feeder from squirrels. Some baffles prevent entry from above or below by creating a slick surface that squirrels cannot climb.

Once you've decided on a type of bird feeder, consider these factors of quality and safety when making or purchasing your feeder.

■ Good materials: Porous materials such as cloth, vinyl, and "netted" metal feeders are more susceptible to moisture, which allows seeds to spoil. Look for solid metal, plastic, wood, or ceramic feeders or cover porous feeders with a plastic dome.

■ Drainage: Water may get into even the most airtight feeders through feeding holes. Drainage holes at the bottom of feeder parts will help this water escape.

■ Capacity: This depends on the kind of birds you want to attract. More specialized feeders such as hummingbird feeders can be smaller, but a feeder frequented by a variety of birds should have a higher capacity. If your feeders are emptying too quickly, it might be time to upgrade.

Downy Woodpecker and Red-breasted Nuthatch on a suet feeder.

■ Sharp edges: Keep an eye out for sharp corners or stray wires that may stab or snare a bird.

Feeder placement

Think about where you want to watch your birds. Your feeder(s) should be visible from this position. Pick a location either within 3 feet from a window, so that birds cannot build up enough momentum, or far away from windows in proximity to trees that may be used as refuge. Providing multiple feeders in different areas of your yard will disperse bird activity. For more information on avoiding window collisions, check the Safety First section of this guide.

Feeder care

Clean your feeders every 1-2 weeks to prevent buildup of droppings, leftover food, and seed hulls. Moldy or spoiled food can make birds sick. Buildup under your feeders can also be bad for ground-foraging birds and pets and may attract unwanted pests.

Wash feeders in hot soapy water or in a solution of 1 part bleach to 9 parts water to disinfect them. Make sure feeders are completely dry before refilling them. Specialty feeders may require different cleaning instructions. For example, the sugary mixture in hummingbird feeders needs to be changed every 3-5 days to prevent fermentation or mold, and the feeders themselves should be cleaned at least once a week. Check your feeder's instructions for more detailed cleaning directions.

WILDBIRDS UNLIMITED

Other materials can attract birds too. You can make your own ball of yarn to include yarn pieces or bits of stuffing for birds to help make their nest. Don't include bright colors that may attract predators to the nest."

BIRD FOOD

The type of food you should feed birds depends on the bird species you want to attract to your yard or other space, ease of cleanup, and season of the year.

Sunflower seeds are a favorite among most birds. Black oil sunflower seeds are easy to crack and rich in fat, while striped sunflower seeds are harder to crack and are better suited for larger birds, such as jays and flickers, and squirrels. All sunflower seeds will attract a variety of birds but are also highly desirable to squirrels. They can be served in a tube feeder or hopper feeder. You can get sunflower seeds in-shell or hulled (shell has been removed). Hulled seeds are great if you don't want shells to accumulate under your feeder, but they are more prone to spoiling, so only put out as much as birds can eat within a few days.

BIRDS IT ATTRACTS
- wide variety of seed-eating bird species

White millet is another favorite of birds. It is high in starch and best for birds that prefer feeding on the ground. It can be offered in a tray or platform feeder, scattered on the ground, or grown in a garden. An added plus of this grain is that squirrels are not particularly interested in millet.

BIRDS IT ATTRACTS
- doves
- some sparrows
- juncos
- buntings
- cowbird

Safflower is perfect if you don't want to attract squirrels to the feeder. Grackles and starlings also don't prefer this seed. It has a hard shell, so it mostly attracts large-billed birds.

BIRDS IT ATTRACTS
- doves
- chickadees
- nuthatches
- finches

Cracked corn is particularly good for ground-feeding birds. It is inexpensive, which makes it a good way to divert certain birds from eating as many of your expensive seeds. However, corn is also attractive to animals such as geese, raccoons, bears, and deer, which you may not want in your yard or other space. It also spoils quickly when wet. A good strategy with corn is to scatter a small amount on the ground each day, or offer it in a tray or platform feeder where pest animals cannot reach it. Never serve red-dyed corn, as it is marked for planting and is toxic to birds.

BIRDS IT ATTRACTS
- doves
- jays
- juncos

Attract Bullock's Orioles with fruit!

LOUIS B. MOOI

Peanuts are another food that is popular among birds. It can be offered in the shell in a specialized tube, tray, or platform feeder, or unshelled in birdseed mixes.

BIRDS IT ATTRACTS
- woodpeckers
- chickadees
- jays

Niger thistle is another seed that squirrels don't like. It is rich in oil and favored by small birds. It can be offered in a specialized finch feeder with a tray to catch the small seeds.

BIRDS IT ATTRACTS
- chickadees
- some sparrows
- juncos
- finches

Nectar is most commonly used to feed hummingbirds, but it attracts other birds as well. A good nectar recipe is 4 parts water to 1 part refined sugar. Never add red dye or use any other type of sugar, honey, or sweetener. This can be deadly to birds.

BIRDS IT ATTRACTS
- hummingbirds
- woodpeckers
- orioles
- finches

Fruit such as orange halves, raisins, berries, chopped apples, and other fruits can be offered in a variety of ways. They can be skewered on special fruit feeders or served in dishes with holes for drainage. They will attract a variety of colorful birds, but be careful to remove them before they begin to rot or mold.

BIRDS IT ATTRACTS
- woodpeckers
- jays
- robins
- waxwings
- tanagers
- orioles

Suet is hardened beef or mutton fat. It is easily digested, an important source of energy, and best for winter feeding since it spoils quickly in warmer temperatures ("rendered" suet doesn't spoil as quickly). In addition, soft suet can coat belly feathers, which can endanger eggs being incubated. Keep suet refrigerated until it is served. Other ingredients such as seeds, nuts, fruit, or insects (good for attracting insectivorous birds) are sometimes added to the fat. Many stores offer special suet feeders, but if you want to reduce the number of starlings eating your suet, find a suet feeder that requires birds to hang upside down to feed.

BIRDS IT ATTRACTS
- woodpeckers
- jays
- chickadees
- creepers
- nuthatches
- wrens

Mealworms provide a source of vitamins, protein, and calcium for the birds that eat them. They may attract many birds that you otherwise wouldn't see at your feeders. You can buy live or freeze-dried mealworms. Keep live mealworms you intend to feed to birds in the bottom of a wide container filled with an inch or so of wheat bran or dry oatmeal with chunks of apple or potato as a source of water. Keep mealworms in a cool place in your house. Freeze-dried mealworms can be easier to maintain and offer to birds. Serve a small amount of mealworms in tray feeders without drainage, as they can escape through these holes. If you want to provide mealworms to only select birds, look for a specialty feeder.

BIRDS IT ATTRACTS
■ kestrels
■ chickadees
■ nuthatches
■ wrens
■ robins

Grit is essential for bird digestion. Grit is used to break down food in the stomach. It will eventually get ground down and digested itself, so grit must constantly be replaced. You can provide grit in the form of a cuttlefish bone, available at any pet store, or broken, cooked eggshells. Offer small eggshell pieces in a shallow dish or platform feeder.

Junk seed including golden millet, red millet, milo, wheat, oats, flax, and other cheap seeds are often used as fillers in commercial birdseed. Watch out for these in mixes since most birds will not eat them. As a consequence, they will spoil more easily and potentially grow weeds under the feeder.

Sometimes predators such as this Cooper's Hawk frequent bird feeders to prey on the songbirds. If this is a common occurrence it would be best to take the feeder down for a few days.

MAGNUS MANSI

WATER SOURCES

Providing a consistent supply of water will assist you in ensuring one
of the basic elements of life for birds is available in your bird sanctuary.
Birds need it for drinking and bathing. Water will also attract non-seed-
eating bird species that you may not be able to attract by birdseed alone.
Birdbaths come in many styles, sizes, shapes, and materials. Before
choosing a birdbath, consider convenience, care, location, and what you
prefer in your yard or other space.

Location
You should consider the location of your bird bath with the same
considerations as you would for a feeder (see page 41), as you want to keep
the visiting birds safe!

Size
Smaller baths are more convenient to clean but have less capacity to
hold more birds. You may want to choose a bath according to the size of
your yard. For example, choosing a large bath can stand out too much
in a small garden or yard. Alternatively, a bath too small will get lost in a
large garden.

Features to consider when selecting a birdbath include:

■ Lip width: What size birds are you hoping to attract? If you want smaller birds, pick a bath with a narrow bowl lip on which the birds can perch.

■ Bowl depth: Do not put out bowls in which birds can drown. Birdbaths should not be more than 1-2 inches deep. If the bath is deeper, put protruding rocks in the water, so if a bird were to fall in the bath it would have a means to get out.

■ Moving water: Birdbaths without moving water tend to attract mosquitoes and accumulate algae. Moving water can be accomplished by a dripper, water spray, bubbler, or fountain and can dramatically increase the number of birds that you attract. Pump kits or other contraptions that move around water are inexpensive and easy to find and install. You'll need a power source for these, however, which may limit where you put the water feature. Consider a solar panel to supply the energy for the pump.

Moving water is a great way to attract birds like this chickadee.

■ Heated bath for the winter: It gets cold along the Front Range during the winter. Unfrozen water during this season can be harder for birds to find. A heater will keep that water flowing and the birds coming!

Materials

Birdbaths can be made using various materials, most commonly cement or plastic. One thing to consider is birds prefer surfaces they can grip. Slippery surfaces, such as those that are glazed, make it easy for birds to lose their footing.

DEVRA COOPER

Few birds prefer to use birdhouses. Some species that typically use tree cavities will also uses man-made structures. These species include kestrels, screech owls, flickers, swallows, chickadees, wrens, and bluebirds. While each of these birds has specific needs, such as house size, height off the ground, hole diameter, and suitable nesting location, they all agree the house should be have the following:

- holes for ventilation at the top and good drainage at the bottom

- sloped roof for protection from the rain and predators

- baffle for protection from predators such as raccoons, cats, and snakes

- rough or grooved interior wall under the entrance to help young birds climb out

Eastern Screech-Owl entering a nest box.

- material of thick, untreated wood that provides insulation

Houses should be put out before the breeding season begins. Along the Front Range, that could be as early as March. Avoid putting birdhouses in areas of your yard where you commonly spray pesticides, which are harmful to birds.

Preventing House Sparrows and European Starlings

It is strongly suggested you take measures to prevent these nonnative species from taking up residence in your birdhouses. These birds were introduced to North America from Europe. As generalists, they out-compete and kill other native bird species' eggs and nestlings. Because these species are not native and therefore not protected under the International Migratory Bird Act, you are allowed to remove any nest material they bring to the box. These birds are diligent, however, so you must be diligent as well by removing material every few days until they move elsewhere.

Birding 101
BE A RESPONSIBLE, RESPECTFUL BIRDER

Bird-watching can be quite exciting! It may create an eagerness in you to watch a bird for a long time or travel a little farther to continue watching a bird that keeps flying away from you. But before you travel too far, please remember basic birding ethics and etiquette.

Ethics
- Always consider the welfare of birds.
- Be silent and observe from a distance. Birds are more likely to come around if you are quiet and not too close to their feeding or nesting areas.
- If you find a nest, do not disturb it. View the nest at a distance. Nestlings may be present in the nest that are not quite developed enough to leave it but will jump if they feel threatened. Also, getting closer and paying more attention to a nest may attract potential predators.

Etiquette
- If you are in a public space, avoid high traffic areas so that others don't have to walk, jog, or bike around you. However, do not tromp around in fragile habitats.
- Do not trespass on private property to observe birds.
- Respect privacy. Avoid pointing your binoculars at other people or at houses.
- Leave no trace. Do not leave trash in parks, open spaces and natural areas.

Get to Know the Birds of the Front Range

Now that you've created a bird sanctuary in your backyard, you can enjoy the birds that visit and live there. The following species profiles include identification tips and habitat information for 55 of the more common backyard bird species found along the Front Range. Note that not all bird species found along the Front Range are included in this guide.

The profiles are organized according to their relationship with each other (hawks are grouped together, sparrows are grouped together, etc.). The emphasis is on adult birds in the breeding (summer) season; many species look different when they are young (first year of life) or during different seasons. In addition, some of these species do not occur year-round along the Front Range. You may only see a species for a day or a week as it passes

through during spring and fall migration. You will surely be kept on your toes as you try to find these migrant species!

JEFF BIREK

If you'd like to see migrant birds and do not have luck in your backyard, you can visit

one of Bird Conservancy of the Rockies' bird banding stations, found in different locations along the Front Range. Visit www.birdconservancy. org for more information.

Each bird species profile includes:

- *Identification Tips:* physical features and sounds of the adult bird that you should be looking and listening for to identify it

- *Timing:* when the species can be found along the Front Range

- *Diet:* what the species likes to eat and what you can provide to attract this bird

- *Conservation Tips:* suggestions of actions you can take in your bird sanctuary to promote the occurrence of this species

We included descriptions of four non-native species commonly seen along the Front Range at the end of our species profiles. These species often compete with our native species and are undesirable. If possible, you should not allow these species to nest in your yard.

TURKEY VULTURE

Identification Tips:

- Body – very large with long robust wings and tail; wings have long feathers that look like fingers on the tips of the wings and make a distinctive "V" shape while in flight

- Color – black or dark brown with a red, featherless head and light-colored bill; on the underside of the wings, flight feathers are paler than other feathers

- Sound – usually does not make much noise but emits low, raspy hisses when agitated

- Other tip(s) – often "teeters" while in flight

Timing: spring and summer

Diet: dead animals

Conservation Tips: Often found in open areas with access to food such as roadsides or landfills, Turkey Vultures can be poisoned by toxins or poisons that accumulate in their prey, especially lead shot left in carcasses by hunters, which can lead to lead poisoning. They often use nests repeatedly and tend to nest away from humans in caves, ledges, and old nests and burrows of other animals.

Identification Tips:

- Body – small agile hawk with small rounded head, short rounded wings, and long square-tipped tail; sexes look alike, but females are larger than males

- Color – adult has blue-gray on the back and wings, gray-capped head with an orange or red eye, and white breast and belly with rusty horizontal barring; juvenile has brown on the back and wings, head streaked brown and white with a yellow eye, and coarse brown streaks on white chest

- Sound – rapid, high-pitched *kik-kik-kik-kik* call

- Other tip(s) – often found among thick woods hunting from lower perches

CORNELL LAB OF ORNITHOLOGY

Timing: year-round

Diet: primarily birds, but occasionally small mammals

Conservation Tips: Sharp-shinned Hawks require thick forests for breeding and have a preference for conifer trees when looking for nest-building sites. They prey mostly on small songbirds and have been known to hunt at feeders.

JON L

COOPER'S HAWK

Identification Tips:

- Body – medium-sized hawk with relatively large head, broad rounded wings, and long rounded tail; this tail, along with its larger size, can help distinguish it from the similar looking Sharp-Shinned Hawk

- Color – adult has bluish-gray on back and wings, large head with a dark gray flattened crown and red eye, and white breast and belly with horizontal reddish bars; juvenile has brown on the back and wings, head streaked brown and white with a yellow eye, and white breast and belly with thin dark streaks; sexes look alike, but females are larger than male

- Sound – raspy, loud *cak-cak-cak* call often heard at nesting sites

- Other tips(s) – found more commonly in open areas than Sharp-shinned Hawks

Timing: year-round

Diet: birds and small mammals

Conservation Tips: Cooper's Hawks can be found in forests, as well as suburbs with enough trees present. These birds prey on medium-sized songbirds such as Rock Pigeons and Mourning Doves, which would expla their high population levels in urban and suburban areas.

JOHN CARR

RED-TAILED HAWK

Identification Tips:

- Body – large soaring hawk with broad rounded wings and short wide tail

- Color – variable, but typically brown above and paler below with brown-streaked band across white belly; adults of all color variations have a distinctive reddish tail that may be pale orange to brick-red, with a black band near the tip; juveniles have typically brown tail with darker bands

- Sound – distinctive, hoarse scream of *kee-eee-arr* that descends at the end

- Other tip(s) – often seen soaring high above fields in a circular pattern, or perched atop telephone poles

Timing: year-round

Diet: small mammals, birds, and snakes

Conservation Tips: Red-tailed Hawks are found in almost all open habitats. They nest on tall trees, cliffs, or other structures. Populations of these birds have been increasing through much of their range.

AMERICAN KESTREL

Identification Tips:

- Body – smallest North American falcon with boldly patterned head, slender pointed wings, and long square-tipped tail

- Color – adult male has blue-gray wings, reddish-brown back with black markings, and rusty tail with black band at tip; adult female is all rufous above with black barring including tail; heads of both sexes have a pair of black vertical stripes on each side of white cheeks

EDUARDO LUGO

- Sound – loud, distinctive *klee-klee-klee*

Timing: year-round

Diet: mainly large insects, but also small mammals, birds, small snakes, and lizards

Conservation Tips:
American Kestrels favor open habitats, such as meadows, farm fields, and grasslands, but need either sparse trees or other structures for nest cavities. Preserve snags (dead trees) with cavities and erect nest boxes, which are readily used. Minimize your use of pesticides that destroy insects and other prey on which kestrels depend.

CORNELL LAB OF ORNITHOLOGY

MOURNING DOVE

Identification Tips:

- Body – medium-sized dove with small head, slender body, and long tapered tail

- Color –grayish-brown plumage overall with black spots on darker wings; in flight, distinctive wedge-shaped tail shows white tips with black borders; male has iridescent blue and pink on the hind neck and pinkish wash on the breast

- Sound – mournful cooing that sounds like *coo-OO-oo, coo-coo-coo*

- Other tip(s) – wings make a fluttering whistle when bird takes flight

Timing: year-round

Diet: seeds and grains

Conservation Tips: Mourning Doves are a very common, widespread bird in open habitats including meadows and grasslands, cultivated fields, and farmyards. These birds frequent backyard feeders in towns and suburbs, so spread millet and cracked corn on the ground or in a platform feeder.

DEANNA BEUTL

GREAT HORNED OWL

Identification Tips:

- Body – large stocky owl with prominent ear tufts (hence its name) and large yellow eyes set in tawny or gray-brown facial disc rimmed with blac

- Color –typically brown or gray plumage, heavily patterned for camoufla on the back and densely barred on breast and belly, with white throat prominent when vocalizing

- Sound – hooting in a series of 3 to 8 low, soft hoots; male and female pa will often perform a duet of alternating hoots

- Other tip(s) –nocturnal bird often seen perched on tree limbs, posts, or other large structures around dusk

Timing: year-round

Diet: rabbits, rodents, birds, and large insects

Conservation Tips: Great Horned Owls are a common bird found in various types of forests often near open habitats. They often nest in old nes of other species in cottonwood, pine, or beech trees. In more desert-like areas, these birds may use cliffs or juniper trees for nesting. They adapt wel if nest sites are preserved and can sometimes be poisoned by pesticides or toxins that have built up in prey.

CORNELL LAB OF ORNITHOLOGY

EASTERN SCREECH-OWL

Identification Tips:

- Body – small stocky owl with large head with short ear tufts and yellow eyes, rounded wings, and short square tail

- Color – gray or reddish-brown (and occasionally brownish) plumage, patterned with dark streaks and intricate bands that allow it to blend in with tree bark

- Sound – spooky, whinnying call that descends in pitch; also long, single trill on one pitch

- Other tip(s) – nocturnal bird more often heard than seen

Timing: year-round

Diet: insects, small mammals, and birds

Conservation Tips: Preserve trees with cavities for nesting and roosting. They will readily use appropriately designed nest boxes to raise young in summer and roost in winter.

ROBERT MARTIN

BROAD-TAILED HUMMINGBIRD

Identification Tips:

- Body – tiny bird that is medium-sized for a hummingbird, with very long bill and broad tail

- Color – metallic green above and white below; male has pinkish-red throat and green sides; female has white, dark-speckled throat and buffy cinnamon sides

- Sound – variety of high-pitched chirps and chitters

- Other tip(s) – males produce a buzzing whirr with their wings

Timing: spring and summer

Diet: nectar and insects

Conservation Tips: Broad-tailed Hummingbirds are found at high elevations in the Rocky Mountains and prefer pinyon, juniper, oak, or pine forests. These birds feed on nectar from red columbines, Indian paintbrush, sage, and pussywillows, as well as sugar water from feeders. Due to their high speed during flight, collisions with windows and cars are a concern for these birds, so reflectors are recommended if putting feeders close to homes.

Identification Tips:

- Body – large distinctive woodpecker with rounded head, long slightly down-curved bill, and fairly long, stiff, tapered tail

- Color – brown plumage overall, with black bars on the back and wings and black spots on the breast and belly; upper breast with conspicuous black crescent bib; bright white rump and red (western race) or yellow (eastern race) underwings visible in flight

- Sound – rapid series of loud wicks and single-note *keeyer*

- Other tip(s) – often found on the ground feeding on insects unlike other woodpeckers

Timing: year-round

Diet: insects (especially ants) and berries

BILL SCHMOKER

Conservation Tips: Preserve trees for nest cavities. Plant berry-producing trees and shrubs. Provide suet in winter. Northern Flickers will use a flicker nest box, but it should be mounted 10-15 feet high.

HERIBERTO VERDUGO-MUNG

DOWNY WOODPECKER

Identification Tips:

- Body –small black-and-white woodpecker with short straight bill that has conspicuous "downy" tuft at the base

- Color – black-and-white plumage above and all white below; head is boldly striped, the male with a red spot at the back; distinguished from Hairy Woodpecker by its smaller size, smaller bill, and spotted outer tail feathers

- Sound – rapid, descending whinny and flat *pik*

Timing: year-round

Diet: insects and berries

Conservation Tips: Preserve trees for foraging and nest cavities. Plant berry-producing trees and shrubs. Provide suet and sunflower seeds in winter.

HAIRY WOODPECKER

Identification Tips:

■ Body – looks like a larger version of the Downy Woodpecker with squarish head and much longer, chisel-like bill

■ Color – black-and-white plumage above and all white below; head is boldly striped, the male with a red spot at the back; distinguished from the Downy Woodpecker by its larger size, longer bill, and unspotted white tail feathers

■ Sound – sharper, higher-pitched peek than Downy Woodpecker call and rapid rattle on one pitch

Timing: year-round

Diet: insects, plus seeds and nuts in winter

Conservation Tips:
Preserve large trees and dead trees and dead limbs in live trees, provided they do not present a safety hazard. Provide suet, peanuts, and sunflower seeds in winter.

NORMAN DOUGAN

JEFF BIR

WESTERN WOOD-PEWEE

Identification Tips:

- Body – medium-sized flycatcher with large head and long pointed wings
- Color – dark brownish-gray plumage above and paler below, with a darker wash on the breast and sides
- Sound – burry, descending *PEE-eer song*

Timing: spring and summer

Diet: insects

Conservation Tips: Western Wood-Pewees are found in open woods especially near water. Loss of wintering grounds in tropical forests has led to declines in this species. Minimize pesticide use.

GARY BOTELLO

SAY'S PHOEBE

Identification Tips:

- Body – medium-sized flycatcher with slender body, flattened black bill, and long black tail

- Color – grayish-brown plumage above, with pale gray throat and breast; buffy-cinnamon belly and undertail

- Sound: descending *pit-see-eur* followed by a rising *chur-eep* for song

Timing: spring and summer

Diet: insects

Conservation Tips: Say's Phoebes breed in open habitats such as grasslands and shrublands, commonly nesting on human-made structures such as bridges, building ledges, sheds, and porches. Minimize pesticide use.

WARBLING VIREO

Identification Tips:

- Body – small chunky songbird with rounded head and short thick bill slightly hooked at the tip

- Color – very plain, unmarked plumage that is dull gray, washed brownish, or olive; whitish below with buffy-yellow sides; white eyebrow contrasts with darker gray crown

- Sound – bubbly, rapid, warble song that typically ends with a higher-pitched note

Timing: spring and summer

Diet: insects, primarily caterpillars, and occasionally berries

Conservation Tips: Warbling Vireos are found in old and new growth deciduous forests, often near a water source, as well as recently cleared coniferous forests where deciduous trees have started growing. They can also be found in urban parks and neighborhoods.

JULIE PRICE

BLUE JAY

Identification Tips:

- Body – large blue songbird with distinctive crest and long rounded tail

- Color – blue back and blue, crested head with white face; wings and tail blue with black bars and white spots; breast pale gray with black necklace; whitish belly

- Sound – harsh, descending *jaaay* and musical whistled *too-li-li* call

- Other tip(s) – known to mimic calls of local hawks

Timing: year-round

Diet: primarily acorns and other nuts and seeds; also insects, small birds, reptiles, and dead animals

Conservation Tips: Provide peanuts, seeds, and suet on platform feeders. Preserve trees for nest building.

KATHIE JOHNSTC

WESTERN SCRUB-JAY

Identification Tips:

- Body – large blue jay with rounded (not crested) head and long tail

- Color – head blue with gray cheek, white eyebrow, and white throat; wings and tail blue; back gray and undersides pale gray with blue breast band

- Sound – extremely vocal with raspy, harsh call

Timing: year-round

Diet: primarily insects and fruit in warm months; acorns and other seeds in cold months; also nestling birds, bird eggs, and reptiles

Conservation Tips: Preserve dense shrubs and small trees for nest building. Provide sunflower seeds and peanuts at feeders.

BILL SCHMOKER

BLACK-BILLED MAGPIE

Identification Tips:

- Body – large black-and-white member of crow family, with very long, diamond-shaped tail

- Color – black head and back with white shoulders and belly; iridescent blue-green on the wings and tail; bright white wing patches flash in flight

- Sound – whiny, nasal *maaag* call that rises in pitch, plus loud raspy chatter

Timing: year-round

Diet: primarily insects and carrion; also berries and seeds

Conservation Tips: Black-billed Magpie nests are large and take as many as 40 days to build. Often found near rivers, these birds can be seen in meadows and sagebrush plains, as well as barnyards and fields where food is readily available.

BILL SCHMOK[E]

AMERICAN CROW

Identification Tips:

- Body – large bird with thick sturdy bill, broad rounded wings, and short rounded tail

- Color – all black plumage and black bill, legs, and feet

- Sound – series of loud caws, sometimes with rattles, croaks, and other sounds

- Other tip(s) – often found in large flocks because of their highly social behavior

Timing: year-round

Diet: vast array of plant and animal food, including insects, grains, seeds, nuts, fruits, and berries; also small birds, mammals, reptiles, bird eggs and nestlings, carrion, and garbage

Conservation Tips: American Crows are common birds native to grasslands and forests. They thrive around people and are often found in parking lots, landfills, backyards, and roadsides often eating roadkill.

WALLACE KECK

COMMON RAVEN

Identification Tips:

- Body – very large bird with large heavy bill, characteristic wedge-shaped tail, and feathers on the throat that give it a shaggy appearance

- Color – all black plumage and black eyes, feet, and bill

- Sound – deep, gurgling, croak-like call

Timing: year-round

Diet: primarily dead animals; also small birds, mammals, reptiles, and bird eggs

Conservation Tips: Common Ravens can be found in many areas including forests and grasslands. These birds do particularly well around people in rural settings but also can be found in cities.

HORNED LARK

Identification Tips:

- Body – medium-sized songbird with distinctive head pattern, short dark bill, and longish wings

- Color – brown back and wings with white breast and belly; head brown and pale yellow with black mask and black "horns" that are often difficult to see; black crescent bib below the throat

- Sound – series of rapid, high-pitched "tinkling" notes that rise in pitch for song; high, lisping chip note for call

Timing: spring and summer

Diet: seeds and insects

Conservation Tips: Horned Larks prefer areas with very short vegetation and bare ground, including prairies, agricultural fields, and heavily grazed pastures. Maintain open grasslands and control encroaching trees and shrubs. Minimize pesticide use.

BRYCE BRADFORD

CLIFF SWALLOW

Identification Tips:

- Body – small compact swallow with small head, very short neck, broad pointed wings, and short square tail

- Color – glossy, dark blue back with white vertical stripes; head with blue crown, dark chestnut face, and bright white forehead; buffy collar and pale orange rump; white belly

- Sound – long string of grating squeaks for song; soft, grating *churr* for call

- Other tip(s) – often seen acrobatically flying high in the air feeding on insects

Timing: spring and summer

Diet: insects

Conservation Tips: Cliff Swallows are locally common in open areas with a water source. They are social birds that nest in colonies, building gourd-shaped mud nests on cliffs and buildings and under bridges and highway overpasses. Minimize use of pesticides.

JOY KEOW

BARN SWALLOW

Identification Tips:

- Body – small slender swallow with long pointed wings and long deeply forked tail

- Color – deep iridescent blue plumage on the back, wings, and tail; crown and face blue with a dark cinnamon throat and forehead; undersides range from rich cinnamon or tawny (males) to pale orange or buff (females) to whitish (juveniles)

- Sound – long series of warbling twitters interspersed with raspy whirrs and nasal rattles for song; squeaky cheeps and whistles for call

- Other tip(s) – often seen acrobatically capturing insects in mid-air

Timing: spring and summer

Diet: primarily large, flying insects

Conservation Tips: Barn Swallows are common birds found in many habitats and elevations. They require open areas for aerial foraging and suitable nesting sites and access to mud for nest building. They prefer human-made structures for nesting, including barns, sheds, stables, and bridges. In spring and summer, leave a window or door open on a suitable outbuilding to encourage nesting. Provide a source of mud.

JOHN CARR

BLACK-CAPPED CHICKADEE

Identification Tips:

- Body – small, plump, large-headed bird with small black bill and long tail

- Color – gray back and tail; wings gray with white edging; head with a black cap, white face, and black throat; undersides white with buffy flanks

- Sound – 2 to 3 note whistle sounding like hey, sweetie for song; clear *chick-a-dee-dee-dee* for call

Timing: year-round

Diet: insects and conifer seeds

Conservation Tips: Install nest boxes for nesting and winter roosting (bluebird-style boxes work well but with 1 ⅛-inch opening). Provide sunflower seed, peanuts, and suet at feeders.

BROWN CREEPER

Identification Tips:

- Body – tiny bird with slender decurved (curved down) bill and spiky rigid tail

- Color – patterned brown and buff above for camouflage with white undersides

- Sound – high-pitched, delicate song with series of clear, often jumbled, notes; high, *lispy see-see* and short, high trill for calls

- Other tip(s) – blends in with tree bark as it spirals up tree trunks, probing crevices for insects

Timing: winter

Diet: primarily insects; some seeds in winter

Conservation Tips:
Retain large conifer trees for foraging such as Douglas fir and ponderosa pine. Provide seeds, suet, and peanut butter at feeders.

BILL SCHMOKER

CORNELL LAB OF ORNITHOLOGY

WHITE-BREASTED NUTHATCH

Identification Tips:

- Body – Small plump bird with a large head, long, slightly upturned bill, and short, broad tail.

- Color – gray-blue above and white below, with chestnut sides and undertail. Head bright white with black cap in males and gray in females

- Song – rapid series of nasal notes on one pitch. Most common call is a nasal *yank*.

Timing: year-round.

Diet: insects, but adds seeds and nuts in winter.

Conservation Tips: Provide peanuts and suet in winter and sunflower seeds year-round. Preserve trees with cavities for roosting and nesting, or provide nest boxes.

GREGG KEND[A]

RED-BREASTED NUTHATCH

Identification Tips:

- Body – tiny compact bird with long pointed bill, short stubby tail, and short broad wings

- Color – male has bluish gray above and cinnamon below, head boldly patterned with black cap, white eyebrow, and black eye stripe; female is similar but with gray cap and paler belly

- Sound – monotonous, nasal *yank-yank* call, often described as sounding like a tiny tin horn

- Other tip(s) – often found foraging on the bark of trees, particularly conifers

Timing: primarily winter

Diet: insects, spiders, and caterpillars; conifer seeds in winter

Conservation Tips: Retain dead trees for excavating nest cavities; rarely uses nest boxes. Provide sunflower seeds, peanuts, and suet in winter.

CORNELL LAB OF ORNITHOLOGY

HOUSE WREN

Identification Tips:

- ◼ Body – very small compact bird with long curved bill, short stubby wings, and tail often cocked upward

- ◼ Color – reddish-brown above with darker bars on the wings and tail; plain buffy or gray-brown below

- ◼ Sound – long, bubbly, gurgling warble that rises and falls in pitch for song; scolding chatter for call

Timing: spring and summer

Diet: wide variety of insects and spiders

Conservation Tips: House Wrens are associated with open woodlands and are comfortable around human habitations. Preserve trees with cavities for nesting, or provide nest boxes. Create brush piles for cover and as a source of insect food. Minimize use of pesticides.

BILL SCHMOK

AMERICAN ROBIN

Identification Tips:

- Body – common, relatively large songbird with robust body and long legs and tail

- Color – gray-brown back and wings, darker head with white eye crescents, and reddish-orange breast and belly; males usually darker overall than females, with blackish head and rich rufous breast and belly

- Sound – cheery song comprised of many clear, rising and falling whistles

Timing: year-round

Diet: insects, earthworms, and berries

Conservation Tips: Plant berry-producing trees and shrubs. Provide a birdbath and nesting shelf. American Robins need wet mud (especially clay) for nest construction.

MARIE LEHMANN

GRAY CATBIRD

Identification Tips:

- Body – medium-sized bird with broad rounded wings, long tail, straight narrow bill, and long legs

- Color – uniform gray plumage above and below, with black cap and tail and rusty red feathers under the tail

- Sound – distinctive, cat-like mew for call that gives the bird its name; rambling medley of harsh, squeaky, and nasal notes interspersed with whistled sweet notes for song

- Other tip(s) – ability to mimic the calls of other birds

Timing: spring and fall migration

Diet: insects and berries\

Conservation Tips: Plant fruit-bearing trees and shrubs.

DEANNA BEUT

CEDAR WAXWING

Identification Tips:

- Body – medium-sized bird with large crested head, broad pointed wings, and short square tail

- Color – distinctive warm brown head with pointed crest and black mask; warm brown back and breast with pale yellow belly; plain gray wings with waxy red tips (adults); tail gray with a bright yellow tip

- Sound – high-pitched, buzzy trill and soft, rising whistle for calls

Timing: winter

Diet: fruit year-round; insects in summer

Conservation Tips: Waxwings are vulnerable to window and car collisions as large flocks descend on fruit-bearing trees in yards and along roadsides. Plant fruiting trees and shrubs away from these areas and insta reflective devices on windows to help avoid collisions.

DAWN WILSON

YELLOW-RUMPED WARBLER

Identification Tips:

- Body – larger warbler with round head, stout black bill, and long tail

- Color – gray above with white wing bars; head gray or brownish with yellow throat and crown patch; bright yellow sides and rump; female duller than male

- Sound – slow, loose trill or warble song that may either rise or fall in pitch

Timing: spring and fall migration

Diet: insects and berries

Conservation Tips: Maintain trees for foraging and minimize use of pesticides. Yellow-rumped Warblers sometimes visit feeders and prefer sunflower seeds, raisins, suet, and peanut butter.

E. ANNE WHITEHUI

YELLOW WARBLER

Identification Tips:

- Body – small songbird with rounded head, thin straight bill, and medium-length tail

- Color – yellow plumage overall; plain yellow face with prominent black eye; male has rich chestnut streaks on the breast and sides

- Sound – bubbly warble song that sounds like *sweet sweet sweet I'm so sweet*

Timing: spring and summer

Diet: insects

Conservation Tips: Yellow Warblers are found in thickets of willows and aspen among streams and wetlands. Maintain existing trees and shrubs near water.

ROBERT MARTINEZ

WILSON'S WARBLER

Identification Tips:

- Body – small songbird with small thin bill, long tail, and black eyes
- Color – olive-green plumage above and yellow below; large black eye on plain yellow face; male has black cap
- Sound – rapid chatter song that drops in pitch at the end

Timing: spring and fall migration

Diet: insects

Conservation Tips: Plant and maintain trees for cover and to support insects for food. Minimize use of pesticides.

JEFF B.

YELLOW-BREASTED CHAT

Identification Tips:

- Body – large chunky warbler with long rounded tail, rounded wings, and thick bill

- Color – plain olive-green plumage above; head with white spectacles and moustache; bright yellow throat and breast; white belly

- Sound – assorted whistles, squawks, mews, rattles, sharp chucks, and soft caws for song

Timing: spring and summer

Diet: insects and berries

Conservation Tips: Maintain existing trees and shrubs near water.

STEPHANIE MONTGOMERY

WESTERN TANAGER

Identification Tips:

- Body – small but stocky songbird with long pointed wings and short stout bill

- Color – adult male has yellow with black back, wings, and tail, and bright red head, duller during migration and winter; female has yellow with gray back and wings; both sexes have prominent wing bars, unlike other tanagers

- Sound – short, raspy series of rising and falling phrases for song; quick, rising *prid-id-dit* for call

Timing: spring and fall migration

Diet: insects, berries, and other fruit

Conservation Tips: Preserve conifers for cover and foraging. Provide fresh fruit, especially cut oranges, and a birdbath or pond.

JEFF B[

SPOTTED TOWHEE

Identification Tips:

- Body – large sparrow with stocky body, thick pointed bill, and long tail

- Color – male has black head, black wings with white spots, dark cinnamon flanks, and white belly; female is similar but grayish-brown where the male is black

- Sound – rapid, buzzy trill or more whistled drink your tea for song

- Other tip(s) – often seen foraging in leaf litter

Timing: spring and summer

Diet: insects, seeds, and berries

Conservation Tips: Maintain patches of dense shrubs with lots of leaf litter. Keep cats indoors to prevent predation on ground-foraging towhees

CORNELL LAB OF ORNITHOLOGY

SONG SPARROW

Identification Tips:

- Body – medium-sized sparrow with rounded head, short stout bill, and long rounded tail

- Color – streaky reddish-brown plumage above and below; head striped reddish-brown and gray, with a broad, dark moustache; whitish breast with thick brown streaks that often form a dark central spot

- Sound – variable series of 2 to 3 clear introductory notes followed by a buzzy trill for song, often represented as *maids, maids, put on your tea kettle-kettle-kettle*

Timing: year-round

Diet: insects and seeds

Conservation Tips: Maintain shrubby areas, especially near water.

COLE SCHNEIL

VESPER SPARROW

Identification Tips:

- Body – medium-large sparrow with short stocky bill and round body
- Color – streaked gray and brown plumage overall; head with white eye ring, dark cheek, and white moustache; underside streaked with brown; white outer tail feathers visible in flight
- Sound – 2 to 4 clear whistles followed by trills and chirps

Timing: spring and summer

Diet: insects, grains, and seeds

Conservation Tips: Maintain open grasslands and minimize pesticide use.

JON DELORENZO

WHITE-CROWNED SPARROW

Identification Tips:

- Body – larger sparrow with short pale bill and long tail

- Color – brown plumage above with streaked back and white wing bars; gray underside with brown flanks; head gray with black-and-white striped crown; crown of immature birds is brown and tan

- Sound – songs and calls vary regionally, but range from clear to trilled whistles, as well as varied, single-call notes

Timing: winter

Diet: insects, seeds, and berries

Conservation Tips: Build backyard brush piles for cover. Provide millet, sunflower, and cracked corn spread on the ground.

DARK-EYED JUNCO

Identification Tips:

- Body – medium-sized sparrow with short bill, round head, and long tail

- Color – plumage varies regionally, with several different races found in Colorado in winter; back color may be dark gray, brown, or brownish-gray; head pale or dark gray, brown-gray, or blackish hood; belly white or white with brown, pinkish, or brownish sides; females overall paler and browner than males; white outer tail feathers visible in flight; all forms have pale bills

- Sound – song is a musical trill with several notes, calls include high-pitched chips and tick sounds, often when flying.

Timing: winter

Diet: seeds and insects

Conservation Tips: Dark-eyed Juncos are common in open woods, fields, parks, and backyards and along roadsides in winter. Provide millet, sunflower, cracked corn, and peanut hearts on the ground and on platform feeders.

STEPHANIE MONTGOMERY

BLACK-HEADED GROSBEAK

Identification Tips:

- Body – stocky medium-sized bird with large head and short neck, large triangular bill, and short tail

- Color – adult male is cinnamon-orange with black head and black-and-white wings; female and juvenile are streaked brown above with paler orange chests

- Sound – robin-like song of sweet, whistled notes that rise and fall in pitch; both sexes sing; sharp, distinctive *spik* for call

Timing: spring and summer

Diet: insects, seeds, and berries

Conservation Tips: Black-headed Grosbeaks select varied habitats where water is readily available. Provide trees and shrubs for cover, nesting, and foraging for insects. Plant berry-producing shrubs for food. Provide water and sunflower seeds at feeders.

STEPHANIE MONTGOMI

LAZULI BUNTING

Identification Tips:

- Body – small finch-like songbird with short bill and tail

- Color – breeding adult male has a bright, turquoise blue head and back with darker wings and tail, cinnamon breast, and white belly; female is drab grayish-brown overall with buffy-orange chest and blue tint on shoulders, rump, and tail; both sexes have a conspicuous pair of white (male) or buffy (female) wing bars

- Sound – high-pitched warble song; dry *pik* call

Timing: spring and summer

Diet: insects, fruits, and seeds

Conservation Tips: Lazuli Buntings can be found in a variety of habitats including areas near water and wooded valleys. Provide trees and shrubs for cover, nesting, and foraging for insects. Plant berry-producing shrubs for food. Provide water and seeds at feeders.

CHERI PHILLIPS

WESTERN MEADOWLARK

Identification Tips:

- Body – chunky robin-sized bird with flat head, long pointed bill, and short tail

- Color – back and wings patterned brown and black; bright yellow throat, breast, and belly, with a large black "V" on the breast; white outer tail feathers obvious in flight

- Sound – flute-like series of whistles and gurgling warbles for song; males sing most commonly from fence posts, telephone poles, and power lines; bell-like *chup* or *pluk* for call

Timing: year-round

Diet: insects and seeds

Conservation Tips: Western Meadowlarks are ground-nesting birds found primarily in croplands, native grasslands, and open shrublands. Delay mowing until after mid-July to avoid destroying nests. Minimize pesticide use. Avoid disturbance during the breeding season, as birds will easily abandon nests.

MICHELLE DESROS

RED-WINGED BLACKBIRD

Identification Tips:

- Body – stocky stout blackbird with wide shoulders and skinny cone-lik bill; often appear “hump-backed” while perched
- Color – male is black overall with characteristic red shoulder patches with buffy-yellow border; female is streaked brown overall with a buff eyebrow
- Sound – gurgling *konk-la-ree* song that ends in a high trill
- Other tip(s) – males are very conspicuous in their behavior, often foun on perches singing to attract females

Timing: spring and summer

Diet: insects and seeds

Conservation Tips: Maintain marshes and other wetland areas and wetland vegetation such as willows and cattails.

COMMON GRACKLE

Identification Tips:

- Body – large slender blackbird with long keeled tail, flat head, and long hefty bill; males larger than females

- Color – plumage appears black from a distance, but iridescence obvious at closer range; head glossy violet-blue with yellow eye; bronze body; juvenile plumage all brown with dark eye

- Sound – short, creaky *readle-EEK* song that sounds like a rusty gate; variety of harsh, raspy chucks, squeaks, and whistles for calls

- Other tip(s) – gregarious birds often found in large flocks

Timing: spring and summer

Diet: primarily seeds and grains; also large insects, small birds, mice, crayfish, fish, frogs, and salamanders

Conservation Tips: Common Grackles do well in human-dominated landscapes, especially farms and suburbs. Provide mixed seeds and grains on platform feeders and spread on the ground.

CORNELL LAB OF ORNITHOLOG

BROWN-HEADED COWBIRD

Identification Tips:

- Body – smallish stocky blackbird with short stout bill, pointed wings, and short tail

- Color – male is glossy black with greenish-blue iridescence and brown head; female is dull brown with darker wings and tail

- Sound – gurgling, high-pitched bubble, bubble, *ZEEE* song; rolling chatter for female's call

Timing: spring and summer

Diet: insects, seeds, and grains

Conservation Tips: Brown-headed Cowbirds lay their eggs in the nests of other bird species, which raise the cowbird young as their own. They will visit backyard feeders, and may be discouraged by taking down feeders until the cowbirds move on.

SARAH DRISCOLL

BULLOCK'S ORIOLE

Identification Tips:

- Body – medium-sized songbird with long tail and slender pointed bill

- Color – adult male is bright orange and black with a large, white wing panel; female has grayish back and wings, yellow head and tail, and whitish belly; young male resembles adult female, but with black eye-line and usually a black throat patch

- Sound – series of whistles and rattles for song; single *churt* and rapid chatters for calls

Timing: spring and summer

Diet: insects, berries, and nectar

Conservation Tips: Bullock's Orioles are common in open woodlands with tall trees, especially near water. Maintain existing trees for foraging and for building their characteristic hanging nests. Provide halved oranges and nectar at feeders.

JOHN CAR

HOUSE FINCH

Identification Tips:

- Body – small finch with blunt rounded bill and slightly long, flattened head

- Color – male has brown back, wings, and tail, red and brown head, and red bib and rump, with belly and sides streaked brown; female streaked brown overall

- Sound – lengthy, relatively high-pitched, burry warble song; single-note *cheep* call

Timing: year-round

Diet: seeds, berries, and buds

Conservation Tips: House Finches are commonly found around human habitations in rural, suburban, and urban areas such as backyards and parks. They are common at backyard feeders.

CORNELL LAB OF ORNITHOLOGY

PINE SISKIN

Identification Tips:

- Body – tiny finch with short pointed bill, long pointed wings, and notched tail

- Color – streaked brown and white plumage above and below; wings dark with buffy (females) or yellow (males) wing bars

- Sound – raspy twitters for song; whiny, rising *zreeee* for call

Timing: winter

Diet: seeds and insects

Conservation Tips: Pine Siskins are gregarious birds that flock to feeders in winter. Provide thistle and black-oil or hulled sunflower seed.

CORNELL LAB OF ORNITHOLO

AMERICAN GOLDFINCH

Identification Tips:

- Body – small but stocky finch with pointed conical bill and short notched tail

- Color – breeding male is bright yellow above and below, with black wings and black cap and forehead, much drabber in winter with brownish back, brownish-yellow head and breast, and dull whitish belly; breeding female is paler yellow above and below, with blackish-brown wings, drab grayish-brown in winter

- Sound – lively series of chips, twills, and twitters for song; common call in flight sounds like *per-chick-a-ree* or *po-ta-to-chip*

Timing: year-round

Diet: seeds and insects

Conservation Tips: Plant native milkweed and thistle, which birds use for nest-building. In winter, provide thistle seed (Niger) and sunflower seed at feeders.

BOB CAMP

EURASIAN COLLARED-DOVE (NON-NATIVE)

Identification Tips:

- Body – plump birds with small heads and long broad tails that are squared at the tips

- Color – light brown to gray with white patches on the tail; wing tips darker than the rest of the wing; narrow black ring also present on the back of the neck

- Sound – characteristic 3-syllable call with the middle syllable often drawn out

Timing: year-round

Diet: seeds, insects, and berries

Conservation Tips: Eurasian Collared-Doves are a non-native species spread to North America from the Caribbean. They are native to Eurasia. They favor urban and suburban areas and owe their successful colonization to bird feeders and the planting of trees that offer nesting sites, which they normally prefer to be at least 10 feet above the ground.

BOB CA

ROCK PIGEON (NON-NATIVE)

Identification Tips:

- Body – plump birds with small heads and short legs, pointed broad wings, and wide round tail

- Color – variable coloration, often a blue gray with two black bands on the wings and a black-tipped tail; often feathers on throat are iridescent

- Sound – soft, gurgling 3-syllable *coo* call

Timing: year-round

Diet: seeds and grains

Conservation Tips: Rock Pigeons are a common non-native species that colonized North America from Europe in the 1600s. These birds thrive in urban settings, often eating people's discarded food.

CORNELL LAB OF ORNITHOLOGY

HOUSE SPARROW (NON-NATIVE)

Identification Tips:

- Body – chunky bird with robust chest and large round head; shorter tail and bigger bill than many sparrows that are native to North America

- Color – male is brightly colored, unless found in cities where they are more dull, with a gray head, white cheeks, black throat, and a dark stripe running across the eye; female is plain brown with lighter undersides, brown, black, and tan stripes down the back, and a dull stripe that only runs behind the eye

- Sound – harsh chirps and cheeps

Timing: year-round

Diet: seeds, insects, and berries

Conservation Tips: House Sparrows are a familiar non-native species that requires nest holes in trees or nest boxes to breed and often favors man-made structures to nest in such as streetlights and nooks in buildings. These birds have historically been common around farms and barns, but have been in decline since the recent industrialization of these areas.

MARK ED

EUROPEAN STARLING (NON-NATIVE)

Identification Tips:

- Body – about the size of a blackbird, plump with long beak, short tail, and short triangular wings

- Color – black with purple to green iridescence in summer; brown with white spots in winter; distinctive yellow bill

- Sound – loud whistles or quitter warbles

- Other tip(s) – ability to mimic calls of other birds

Timing: year-round

Diet: insects, berries, and seeds

Conservation Tips: European Starlings are a non-native species originally from Europe that competes with native birds for nest cavities. They often frequent feeders and tend to thrive near humans.

☐ Turkey Vulture (b)
☐ Sharp-shinned Hawk
☐ Cooper's Hawk
☐ Red-tailed Hawk
☐ American Kestrel
☐ Mourning Dove
☐ Great Horned Owl
☐ Eastern Screech-Owl
☐ Broad-tailed Hummingbird (b)
☐ Northern Flicker
☐ Downy Woodpecker
☐ Hairy Woodpecker
☐ Western Wood-Pewee (b)
☐ Say's Phoebe (b)
☐ Warbling Vireo (b)
☐ Blue Jay
☐ Western Scrub-Jay
☐ Black-billed Magpie
☐ American Crow
☐ Common Raven
☐ Horned Lark (b)
☐ Cliff Swallow (b)
☐ Barn Swallow (b)
☐ Black-capped Chickadee
☐ Brown Creeper (w)
☐ White-breasted Nuthatch
☐ Red-breasted Nuthatch (w)
☐ House Wren (b)
☐ American Robin

☐ Gray Catbird (m)
☐ Cedar Waxwing (w)
☐ Yellow-rumped Warbler (m)
☐ Yellow Warbler (b)
☐ Wilson's Warbler (m)
☐ Yellow-breasted Chat (b)
☐ Western Tanager (m)
☐ Spotted Towhee (b)
☐ Song Sparrow
☐ Vesper Sparrow (b)
☐ White-crowned Sparrow (w)
☐ Dark-eyed Junco (w)
☐ Black-headed Grosbeak (b)
☐ Lazuli Bunting (b)
☐ Western Meadowlark
☐ Red-winged Blackbird (b)
☐ Common Grackle (b)
☐ Brown-headed Cowbird (b)
☐ Bullock's Oriole (b)
☐ House Finch
☐ Pine Siskin (w)
☐ American Goldfinch

NON-NATIVE SPECIES
☐ Eurasian Collared-Dove
☐ Rock Pigeon
☐ House Sparrow
☐ European Starling

Migrant only (m), breeding only (b), wintering only (w)

Bird Conservation Resources

FIND OUT OTHER WAYS YOU CAN HELP

Creating a bird sanctuary in your backyard or other space is a great step toward conserving birds. The most serious threat facing birds is habitat loss and destruction, and you've helped to provide habitat for birds. With so many bird species populations in decline, it is more important than ever to do what you can to help conserve our feathered friends. Thank you!

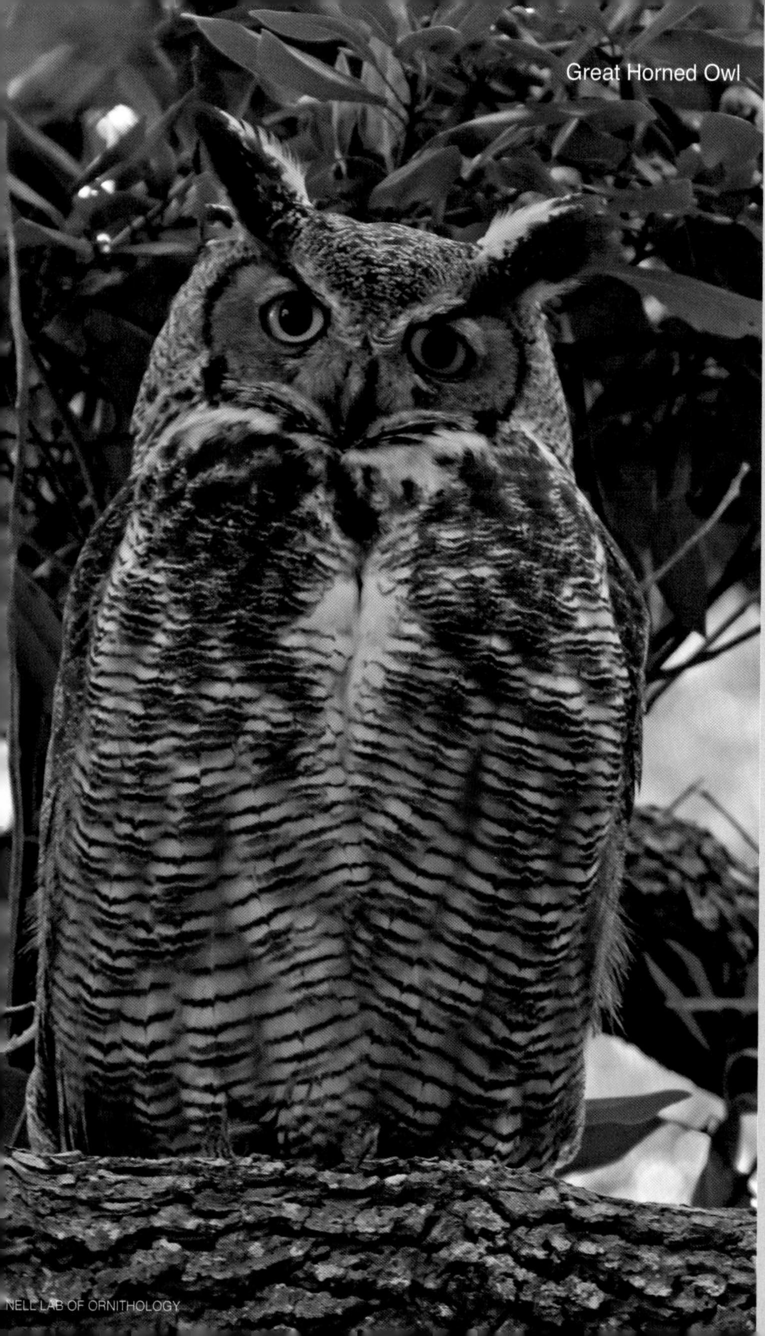

NELL LAB OF ORNITHOLOGY

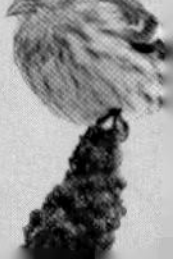

Join a bird conservation organization.

Become an active member of a group that conserves birds and their habitats. Many organizations, such as Bird Conservancy of the  Rockies, do critical work to protect, restore, or enhance habitat for birds and other wildlife.

Participate in citizen science projects.

Make a difference by observing nature and sharing your information. Many organizations, such as Bird Conservancy of the Rockies, offer opportunities to participate in real science – some of which can occur in your backyard or local area – that helps to guide conservation efforts for birds and other wildlife.

Educate others about birds.

Talk to your children, other family members, and friends about the need to conserve birds, or become a trained educator and volunteer. Many organizations, such as Bird Conservancy of the Rockies, offer volunteer naturalist programs.

Work with your neighbors.

Continue the conversation with those who live near you. Together, you can create an even larger habitat for birds in your neighborhood.

Write to your politicians.

Let your local, state and national political leaders know that you care about the future of our birds. Encourage them to be concerned about habitat loss.

SHARE YOUR KNOWLEDGE!

As you develop your bird sanctuary, you can become an inspiration for others and educate them about what you've learned. Your yard or other space can offer engaging, hands-on learning for people of all ages. Nature is a powerful teacher, especially for children. The direct experiences you, your family, and friends have in the environment you've create helps foster awareness and appreciation of our natural world. It may also offer insight into how fragile it can be and how, when pieces are taken out or added in, it can affect how everything else operates.

OTHER RESOURCES

If you are looking for additional information about topics in this guide the following websites direct you.

Native plants/habitat

- Native Plant Society
  http://www.conps.org/
  http://npsnm.unm.edu/
  http://www.wynps.org/
- Audubon Rockies Habitat Heroes
  http://rockies.audubon.org/engagement/habitat-hero-program
- The Center for Resource Conservation
  http://conservationcenter.org/gardens/
- National Wildlife Federation: Garden for Wildlife
  http://www.nwf.org/How-to-Help/Garden-for-Wildlife.aspx
- Lady Bird Johnson Wildflower Center as there are over 8,000 native plants in their database http://www.wildflower.org/plants/
- Colorado State University (CSU) Extension
  - Horticulture Agents & Specialists: http://csuhort.blogspot.com/
  - Colorado Native Plant Master Program Plant Database http://jeffco.us/coopext/intro.jsp
- Wyoming University Extension http://www.uwyo.edu/uwe/programs/
  - Barnyards and Backyards http://www.uwyo.edu/barnbackyard/
- New Mexico State University Extension http://extension.nmsu.edu/
- Botanic Gardens along the Front Range:
  - Hudson Gardens http://www.hudsongardens.org/
  - Denver Botanic Gardens has a "Garden Navigator" that allows you to locate and learn about the plants within their collection. http://navigate.botanicgardens.org/
  - Gardens on Spring Creek http://www.fcgov.com/
  - Cheyenne Botanic Garden http://www.botanic.org/
  - Santa Fe Botanical Gardens http://santafebotanicalgarden.org/
- National Audubon Society http://www.audubon.org/conservation/creating-bird-friendly-communities
- USDA Natural Resources Conservation Service's Plants Database http://plants.usda.gov/java/

Citizen Science

- Cornell Lab of Ornithology (http://www.birds.cornell.edu/) manages 12 bird citizen science programs including
  - Project Feeder Watch
  - NestWatch
  - eBird
  - Great Backyard Bird County
- Bird Conservancy of the Rockies http://www.birdconservancy.org/get-involved/volunteer/citizen-science/
  - Eastern Screech Owl
  - HawkWatch
  - Bald Eagle Watch
  - Colony Watch
- Wyoming Biodiversity Citizen Science Initiative (WyoBio) http://wyobio.org/about/
- National Audubon Society
  - Christmas Bird Count https://www.audubon.org/conservation/science/christmas-bird-count
  - Of Greater Denver—Colorado Bluebird Project http://www.denveraudubon.org/conservation/bluebird-project/
  - Hummingbirds at Home http://www.hummingbirdsathome.org/

Bird Watching

- Colorado Field Ornithologists http://cobirds.org/
- Colorado Birder http://coloradobirder.ning.com/
- Colorado Birding Trail http://coloradobirdingtrail.com/map/
- Colorado County Birding http://coloradocountybirding.org/
- Colorado Birding Society http://coloradobirdingsociety.net16.net/
- Audubon Chapters http://www.audubon.org/audubon-near-you

Find a Wildlife Rehabilitator near you

- http://ahnow.org is a good resource for the Front Range